Mike

Happy Christmas

love

Nanette & Bryan

2000

The Party Blonde

Lady Wildboarclough is a great believer in the virtues of fountain pens, dry sherry and Peter Jones

The Party Blonde

SOCIAL STEREOTYPES FROM THE

Telegraph magazine

Victoria Mather

and

Sue Macartney-Snape

JOHN MURRAY

First published in 2000
by John Murray (Publishers) Ltd,
50 Albemarle Street, London W1X 4BD

A catalogue record for this book is available from the British Library

ISBN 0–7195–6223 6

Typeset in 11.5/15pt Monotype Bembo

Printed and bound by
Canale, Torino, Italy

Introduction

I TELEPHONED VICTORIA Mather to find out when this book would be published. 'Haven't the faintest. Call Sue. Of course I sound miles away. I'm in Los Angeles for the Oscars. Actually, this minute, I'm leaving for Vegas on a private jet. *Love* those two words together. Bye – oh, that bag in the cabin with me, Terry, thank you.' Immediately the image begins to form . . . the private jet attendant . . . Terry, 38, but blonder than he was . . . used to buttle for Princess Michael . . . lives in Teddington (so handy for the airports) with pierced boot-boy Abdul who pattern-cuts for Julian McDonald . . . Sue was in Nepal, painting and untraceable.

How *do* they hit the target every time, achieving such acute perception, these two wunderkinder of the dottily comic? Victoria's always way too high above ground to have her ear glued to it, and Sue Macartney-Snape's eye is *just* too kind to extract the tooth. And yet they consistently shake up the dormant chrysalis of human comedy in some cerebral kaleidoscope. The colourful fragments float down, wings just beating with still resuscitable life, to be captured in the author's butterfly nets and skilfully pinned, but never skewered, on the mounting boards of artistic scrutiny.

The answer lies, of course, in fondness. Never condemning, nor sour, but always *au courant* (*en avance*, even – Victoria was the first person I ever heard utter the words Spice Girls), they paint a written portrait of uniquely English character and caricature, but with no patronizing mock, no Proustian nostalgia. *Their* Madeleine would be an ageing rock-chick gone country – more cambric than Cambrey. As observers, their laser-beam eye socially x-rays the quarry, and then re-clothes it with (often fuller) flesh, warts and all manner of foibles. As writers they create legends. Like Greek myths, or Roman lays, like Saint-Simon at Versailles, or Aubrey, or tales of the Raj, future surfers on stream will log on to *The Party Blonde* and think 'so *that* was England's green and pleasant land.'

It's a rich field to undermine. For while charladies, rag-and-bone men, society hostesses and old buffers – one, younger than I, thought Britney Spears was French asparagus – still exist, Victoria and Sue, ably abetted by Emma Soames, unearth a new archetypal category in the *Daily Telegraph* each Saturday. Saturday? My dear, won't they be in Uruguay, sketching? Or on the private jet? Possibly, but always waiting, watching for the absolutely typical, and utterly topical too.

Nicky Haslam
Autumn 2000

For
EMMA SOAMES
A great woman and a great friend

Six years is a long time in newspaper columns, and there have now been some 350 social stereotypes in the *Telegraph Magazine*, edited by Emma Soames. She and we have been together longer than most modern marriages. This is the third anthology, and many thanks are due to the *Telegraph* readers who have consistently written to encourage us to identify the supporting characters in all our lives.

As the writer, I could not have realised the cast herein without the help with research provided by friends who have far better things to do but have always been unfailingly generous: Max Hastings, the editor who brought me to the *Daily Telegraph* in 1986, Nicholas Coleridge and Christopher Fildes, the lodestars of my writing life. Also Ned Sherrin, Sarah and Johnny Standing, Vernon Colhoun, Kate Reardon, Kiki McDonough, Caroline Wrey, Alexander Walker, Camilla Dempster, Conrad and Barbara Black, and Desmond Lynam. Frank Bowling has given me a second home, along with the Oscar nominee, at the Hotel Bel-Air. Special love, always, to my husband, John Raymond, and my brilliant god-daughter Scarlett Lacey.

As the illustrator, Sue would like to thank Hugh, Annabella, Piers, Eugenia, Thomas, Sarah, George, John, Nicholas, Dora, Andrew, Kitty, Roger and Nancy.

Denis Piggott is our splendid production manager at the *Telegraph*; the column's editor, Louise Carpenter, has fielded both text and illustrations from all over the world; and Caroline Knox's enthusiasm championed the book at John Murray.

V.M. and S. M.-S.
London, November 2000

Margaret has not taken kindly to answering all calls as
'Deutsche Fluid Couplings'

The Telephonist

'PUTTING YOU THROUGH,' intones Margaret as she connects Frankfurt to the chairman's office with grim disapproval. Earlier in the year the company was bought by the Germans, and Margaret has not taken kindly to answering all calls as 'Deutsche Fluid Couplings'. It is part of a conspiracy, along with voicemail, e-mail and direct lines, to make her job more difficult and quite possibly redundant. Margaret has worked at Fluid Couplings for twenty years and takes pride in the personal service she provides: recognising the chairman's wife's voice, remembering extension numbers by heart (although the computer is very handy for the temporary staff) and taking messages from callers pathetically grateful to speak to a person, not a machine. Those who do not recognise her sterling worth in these respects risk having their international calls cut off.

There wasn't all this communication when Margaret first became a telephonist and she is not at all sure she approves of it. As she says to her husband Stanley, communication there may be, but no one is ever *available* any longer. They're 'not at their desk right now', and only the other day the managing director had to dial zero to ask Margaret if she knew where his secretary had got to. Gone to the Café Mocha – really, these girls. The cappuccino has not penetrated the fastness of Margaret's eyrie, which is equipped with a kettle, a catering pack of Lyons teabags and a Princess Diana mug. Also Margaret's knitting, not that she has much time for it these days, nor for many little chats – Mr Craddock in marketing is quite a favourite – because everyone's so busy and cross. It is strange that although Margaret is the company's frontline on communication, no one actually knows where the switchboard is.

The Squire

WILLOUGHBY DAVENPORT HAS just anaesthetised the congregation with St Matthew 37: 'The harvest is truly plenteous, but the labourers are few', declaimed with feeling since his estate workers are eked out by lads with nose studs on youth opportunity schemes.

Life is not as it was in the days of his grandfather, Sir Digby Davenport, now in the adjacent family tomb, peacefully oblivious to inheritance tax and the dry rot in the Jacobean library at Willoughby Park. Will is pink-cheeked with doggedly maintaining the status quo, his elder sibling having absconded to Monte Carlo with the title and a drink problem. He thought that selling Pig's Hollow to Flogitcheep supermarkets would alleviate the pressure on his bank account but local protest groups have made his life a misery and the profit seems to have been swallowed by the arrears in school fees for Charles (now touching him for the money to open a themed restaurant in Brixton) and Edward, who − after all the expense of a public school education − is having to re-take his A-levels at Mander Portman. There was Lloyd's, of course; and then his wife who ran off with little Pandora's piano teacher, preferring a life of aesthetic abandon in Italy to perpetually opening the church fête.

Old Nanny is still at home, thank the Lord, and stoutly backs Willoughby in his struggle with the vicar to have *All Things Bright and Beautiful*, including the line 'The rich man in his castle, the poor man at his gate/God made them high and lowly, he knoweth their estate'. But as Will drives home from church in his shooting-brake (no vulgar 4 × 4s at Willoughby Park) he feels horribly like the poor man at his own gate, and that the point of his earthly struggle is fast being diminished.

Life is not as it was in the days of his grandfather, Sir Digby Davenport, now in the adjacent family tomb, peacefully oblivious to inheritance tax and dry rot in the Jacobean library

*Her innate style was forged by the fantasy of dressing up as a
fairy princess in Fortuny, Worth and Startrite sandals*

The Muse

TATIANA PUFF IS the inspiration for Zorab, the brilliant Croatian designer who has taken haute couture by storm with combat chic. It created the most enormous stir when Tatiana wore a Zorab flak jacket, handwoven in marsh grass and silk, with a Thirties Balenciaga ball dress. When Zorab went to the Camargue, Tatiana was the first to have an evening coat made from the hide of a black bull. Her hats are famous, particularly the cloche she made herself from a shrimping net and seashells gathered on her family's private beach in Cornwall.

The Puffs have owned the house – rambling, covered in ivy and with buckets strategically placed to catch leaks from the roof – for generations. As a child Tatiana played in the attic, where her grandmother's clothes were kept in Vuitton steamer trunks. Here her innate style was forged by the fantasy of dressing up as a fairy princess in Fortuny, Worth and Startrite sandals. Nan Kempner would give her seat on the front rows of the world's catwalks to have Tatiana's consequent ease with fashionable eclecticism. She is not a woman who would ever wear matching shoes and handbag. Nor is her style anything to do with designer labels, an obsession which, if she thought about it at all, Tatiana would regard as mud upon her violet silk Kelian boots.

It is because her style has absolutely nothing to do with fashion that she has been elected a fabulous fashion monument.

The Best Man

JASPER WAS GIVEN a warning salvo by the bride's father. 'Friendly advice, my boy. Don't try to be funny in your speech. Great-Aunt Moira's coming. Devoted to Natasha, no children of her own, got some marvellous jewellery, always been led to believe . . . Well, let's just say it would be better not to upset her.'

Natasha, who hasn't lost the weight she'd hoped and can't do a *thing* with her hair, has already said Jasper is not, on any account, to refer to what went on in the Crazy Horse Saloon during the stag weekend in Paris. Jasper, who has the mild manners of the short-sighted and cerebral, now feels like the really stupid one in *Men Behaving Badly*. At Oxford he was considered rather a wit, having once composed a limerick about Thucydides, and he has known the bridegroom since their nannies used to trundle them towards the Peter Pan statue. Ludgrove, Eton, Christ Church, then sharing a flat, have been the glue of Jasper's and Dominic's friendship. Dominic was the charmer who treated girls appallingly (not to be mentioned in the speech), Jasper the cuddly one who cooked spag bol, kept the laundry at bay and gave weeping Camillas (also unmentionable) tenners for taxis home.

Having stopped Dominic getting drunk at the ushers' lunch, remembered the ring, passports and tickets to Bali, and ambushed the bride's teenage brother putting kippers in the engine of the going-away car, Jasper says his few words absentmindedly clutching the teddy that kept the youngest page subdued in church. His warm portrait of Dominic is guaranteed to placate the fiercest gem-encrusted aunt. Throughout he feels Natasha's eyes boring into his new waistcoat, and realises he's lost a best friend without gaining a sister.

Jasper is not, on any account, to refer to what went on in the
Crazy Horse Saloon during the stag weekend in Paris

'Look what she does for charity, there are orphans who
would be bare-assed without her'

The Manhattan Wife

Mrs Barney Gruzman III has the intractable demeanour of a woman who is above a credit card. The accounts from Bill Blass and Oscar de la Renta are sent to the chairman's office at Gruzman International, where they are Dealt With. Gloria Gruzman's life, apart from blips like Concorde running late, is dealt with in a way which tolerates no mundane imperfections. There is always a table for her at Le Cirque; her house on Long Island has been pictured in *Architectural Digest*; her apartment on East 76th and Fifth Avenue is but two blocks from The Carlyle hotel – where she retreats in domestic crises (like her maid having a cold). Bobby Short, when not playing piano at the Café Carlyle, is the signature of her soirées.

Whether at a patrons' evening at the Metropolitan Museum or at the couture, Mrs Gruzman has trout mouth. This is the inverted slash of scarlet Elizabeth Arden permanently downturned in disapproval. It matches the inverted commas of the helmet hair, and has been perfected to discourage ill-groomed waiters who bring her anything over which garlic has been wafted, and little people of any description who Do Not Know Who She Is.

Barney, who's had a soothing succession of mistresses in Brooklyn, says that Gloria is a wonderful woman who won't take no for an answer. 'Just look what she does for charity, there are orphans who would be bare-assed without her.' Gloria, in fur against the vagaries of air-conditioning, has sprinkled the gold dust of Barney's grocery pile on these unfortunates, but never felt it necessary to see them.

The Wimbledon Lineswoman

CICELY GOSSAGE IS a kindly wife and indulgent grandmother who dotes on her wire-haired dachshund, Banger, but she simply will not put up with nonsense from Stefan Slamovich. He may be the new Russian tennis star, but if she says his ball is out, it is out, and Mrs Gossage is not a woman to be trifled with when her arm shoots sideways. She has dealt with more unpleasant scenes than any precipitated by a deuce call at match point, since she is a magistrate. Streams of Russian invective are as nothing compared with what Cicely Gossage has witnessed visiting remand centres.

Tennis is her passion: a wicked forehand slice ensured her captaincy of the Ladies' Thirds at the Chevening-on-Sea tennis club and she began umpiring minor tournaments in her twenties. Wimbledon is an honour, of course, and she did her time on the outer courts. Bjorn Borg, now he was a gentleman, and there was the day when Ken Rosewall winked at her during the senior doubles. She prefers the men's matches, never really having taken to the women's newfangled habit of grunting and keeping their balls in their knickers. It is not how she played when she was a gel. Only the other day she confided sadly to Banger, during one of their bracing walks on the beach, that grace and femininity departed international tennis the day Evonne Goolagong retired.

And then there's the Cyclops, which Mrs Gossage views with disdain. Nothing mechanical could improve upon her own judgement, forged in the McEnroe years (what a naughty boy he was!). Every muscle, every bone sustaining her foursquare stance, every instinct is poised, positively tingling with concentration when the players serve. Mr Gossage is most concerned that one day she'll be hit by a ball at 140 mph, but she thinks the risk is worth it if Agassi smiles at her just once.

18

Nothing mechanical could improve upon her own judgement,
forged in the McEnroe years

There was once an unfortunate incident when Persimmon confused the swimming-pool's chlorine dose with Slug-It

The Old-fashioned Gardener

PERSIMMON HAS BEEN at Butter Hall since the old baronet's day. There were eight under-gardeners then, now there's just Persimmon accumulating weapons of mass destruction in the potting shed. He drenches the gravel paths with sodium chlorate (jealously stockpiled ever since the herbicide police declared it dangerous to children) and moss deterrents; the bindweed in the yew hedges is ruthlessly sprayed with Shrivel! Now is the time of year when he unleashes vats of slug pellets in the herbaceous borders; the offensive against black spot, greenfly and mildew is being planned in minute detail; and he is ever on the alert for rust among the camellias. The result of this scorched-earth policy is that the battle lines have been eroded between nature and nurture.

In his determination to rid Butter Hall's little Eden of pests and fungi, Persimmon now conducts his pruning with similar vigour. Sir Tertius longs for him to go on holiday with his sister in Ventnor, just so that the roses can have a chance to recover. Last year the magnificent blush-pink Albertine, which had been doing so well in the arbour, was reduced to a stump. The Gloire de Dijon has proffered only timorous yellow buds since Persimmon gave it his undivided attention, a frenzy of activity following her new ladyship's acquisition of a 'garden designer' – a gent in cashmere who wanted to grow peaches around the swimming-pool. Persimmon has never approved of that pool – there was once an unfortunate incident when he confused the chlorine dose with Slug-It. And as for fruit and veg, they should be in the walled garden, and he likes a broad bean to be broad. Her ladyship is always asking for the vegetables to be picked when there's nothing to them. At home in the village, Persimmon grows marrows that win prizes in three counties.

The Oscar Nominee

As ANNA GLIDES up the red carpet at The Shrine, towards the cameras, the lights, the action and Joan Rivers, who will conduct a television interview about her hair extensions, she feels quite unreal. Her dress is borrowed, and has practically had to travel by separate limousine. Come the dawn, her jewellery will revert to Asprey's. Her make-up has been done by Tina (who does Gwyneth), and her room at the Hotel Bel-Air (no 160, Princess Grace's old favourite with its own fountain) is airless with the competing bouquets from her English agent, who discovered her, and her American agent, who has never met her.

Since her nomination for playing the tortured, schizophrenic, blind, lesbian pianist in *Adagio*, Anna has been photographed by Annie Liebowitz for *Vanity Fair*, has lunched with Tom and Nicole at Morton's, and been to drinks at the Sky Bar to meet Quentin Tarantino. There's hardly a moment to think of her traumatic break-up with Jake Rash, drummer with the indie band Penetration. They first looked into each other's eyes over vodkatinis in the Met Bar: she was the new Britflick babe and he and his goatee beard were on the cover of *The Face*. It was a verdant relationship of photo-opportunities but now, when Anna needs him, as she tries to memorise an acceptance speech (it would be bad luck to write it down), he is with a Radio 1 DJ and she's with her mother, Angela, who has only previously ever left Haywards Heath for motoring holidays in France. Although Matt Damon took his mum to the *Vanity Fair* party, Anna is marginally worried as to whether a parent is this year's cool accessory.

Since her nomination for playing the tortured, schizophrenic, blind, lesbian pianist in Adagio, *Anna has been photographed by Annie Liebowitz for* Vanity Fair

Flushed with heat, Geoff is now the Antony Worrall Thompson of the barbie

The Barbecue Host

NEVER KNOWINGLY SEEN in the kitchen, Geoff becomes a tinpot tyrant as soon as a sausage hits the Weber. Armed with a pair of tongs and a salacious apron, he is the hunter-gatherer of Carshalton, yelling instructions about honey and balsamic vinegar marinade to his wife, Anthea, through the kitchen window. She's asked the neighbours round to see the transformation of the garden at Sunnyview with pebbles, fashionable grasses and a water feature.

Unfortunately the barbecue, such a level presence on the old crazy paving, goes all wonky on the pebbles and Geoff lights it too late so clouds of smoke waft over the assembled guests. 'This is the real thing,' he coughs heartily. 'Nothing like it for flavour. Those gas-fired jobs are for poofters.' Anthea hands round the cheese straws, handkerchief pressed to her mouth. The full benefits of the water feature are admired when the kebabs catch fire and are saved only by Shirley Trimingham's mercy dash to the ornamental pond. 'Well done, that Shirl,' cries Geoff, expansively waving a charred pork chop and his glass of wine.

By 10 o'clock everyone is catatonic on Koala Creek merlot and all the crisps have been eaten. 'Now what I need – *Anthea!* – is some soya sauce and crushed garlic. And bring the ketchup while you're about it.' Flushed with heat, Geoff is now the Antony Worrall Thompson of the barbie, an applier of savoury unguents to innocent strips of meat and a man who has a way with corn on the cob in Bacofoil. Anthea has lit little nightlights on the new teak garden furniture from Homebase and, in a last, desperate delaying tactic, produces cocktail onions. 'Come and get it, folks!' shouts Geoff triumphantly. He has laboured mightily and brought forth two carcinogenic chicken breasts.

The Country Opera
Picnickers

Lady Fothergill is heading for the ha-ha with the inexorable determination of Caesar at the head of legions. Behind her, Sir Reginald staggers under a wicker hamper containing pink food: potted shrimps, salmon and strawberries. Their spindly, bespectacled son will bring up the rear with a coldbox of gin and full-leaded tonic as soon as he's parked the car.

Mary Fothergill, a patron of Cherington Opera, always demands to be set down near the wicket gate so she can reach her favourite bench under the oak tree, the herbaceous border to the right and, beyond the ha-ha, cows serenely chewing the cud. Woe betide anyone innocently approaching this pastoral idyll; the Fothergills' *La Traviata* will be ruined if they have to picnic in the knot garden. Thus they always arrive early to defend their position with rugs covered in dog hair and Sir Reginald's shooting stick. While he goes in search of programmes, Lady Fothergill will decant a wobbling ring of tomato mousse from a Tupperware mould and annoint it with watercress. Over the years, much thought has gone into the propriety of having a picnic table, since it involves a second journey to and from the car, but Sir Reginald's rheumatism has ensured the triumph of practicality. He likes knees-under, and it lessens the risk of spilling cream on the rug.

Having had a stiff sharpener before the first act, the Fothergills are prepared to enjoy themselves. Cherington is a splendid little effort, thoroughly deserving of their support – not that they would go to anything sung in German. After the interval Sir Reginald, replete with the salmon and some rather good Montrachet, sleeps blissfully in the stalls, occasionally coming round to ask when that damned woman will stop warbling and die. Packing up afterwards, Lady Fothergill tenderly secretes a cutting from the herbaceous border in some kitchen roll.

The Fothergills' La Traviata *will be ruined if they have to picnic in the knot garden*

Mr Featherstone likes to see his victims personally, breaking the bad news with a sympathetic handshake like a wet sponge

The Bank Manager

MR FEATHERSTONE IS perpetually worried. He would like to be accommodating, he really would, but the whole point of him is that he has been drilled to say no. And things are not what they were at Hogg's, once affectionately known by its clients as the Piggy Bank but now an emasculated subsidiary of the National Allied. Since Lloyd's losses have reduced Hogg's feisty dowagers and retired Army colonels to abject civility, Mr Featherstone rather misses being patronised as a tiresome little man. Only the other day he had to explain to Lady Fanshawe that she really could not afford another hunter, and she was quite meek about it. His grander clients are Mr Featherstone's tangential link with the dizzy world of Nigel Dempster and, over a glass of medium-dry sherry, he discreetly regales his wife Muriel with tales of extravagance unknown in Coulsdon.

But monies to fund corporate entertaining at Annabel's are now eclipsed by the savage thrill of calling in the overdrafts on promising small businesses. Mr Featherstone likes to see his victims personally, breaking the bad news with a sympathetic handshake like a wet sponge. They bitterly remember the day when they first encountered Mr Featherstone's clammy charms and he cracked his one joke about being trained to make advances. What no one understands is that beneath Ernest Featherstone's rayon tie beats a heart gripped by the fear of being replaced by a computer.

*It's the stress that makes her smoke. No one knows
what it's like with the new computer system*

The Office Smoker

SINCE PRODIGAL, PRINGLE and Pratt espoused non-smoking premises, Janice has been forced to descend twenty-eight floors to have a gasper. Clutching her packet of Silk Cut, she stands forlornly in the biting wind, inhaling her furtive pleasure among the office dustbins. Mr Prodigal, a reformed smoker, has decreed that no one can indulge outside the front door, as it might give clients an impression of indolence and sloth unbecoming in a firm of chartered accountants.

Janice has indeed had a little talking to from Mr Pringle, who's worked out that if she smokes six a day, and it takes five minutes to smoke a cigarette, and some seven minutes to go up and down in the lift, Prodigal, Pringle and Pratt is losing half a dozen man hours per week. 'We are considering clawing back this time from your lunch break,' he said severely. 'The firm cannot indulge bad habits.' Janice protested that she would, if she could, smoke out of the window, thus saving the seven minutes in the lift, but everything is hermetically sealed because of the air-conditioning. She tried the stairwell, secreting the butts in an empty box of Swan Vestas, but Lucille from bought ledger reported her to Mr Pratt. So it's the dustbins or nothing.

Hunched against the elements, Janice is sometimes joined by Craig from the postroom and they grind their stubs into the pavement, pretending it is Mr Pringle's face. It's the stress what makes her smoke, innit? No one knows what it's like with the new computer system, and the reports Janice has had to input have been cruel. She's probably got repetitive strain injury by now. They're lucky to have her, they are. That's what she tells her mum and the cat at home in Ealing. Next week Janice'll try to give up, but it's her nerves, see?

He drops ash on the carpet and never knows when to leave

The Husband's Best Friend

DIANA NEARLY REFUSED Andrew's proposal of marriage because she was so terrified he'd ask Jumbo to be his best man. She just knew Jumbo would goose Aunt Violet and make obscene suggestions to her teenage sister in whisky breath: 'Don't you know the chief bridesmaid and the best man are supposed to get off together, little Katie?' Fortunately Andrew chose his brother, Peter, an unimpeach-ably sober accountant. The prospect of a best man's speech of stul-tifying boredom made Diana (and Diana's mother) weak with relief, compared to Jumbo's inevitable rodomontade of Andrew's fictitious sexual aberrance. At least, Diana hopes it's fictitious. Whenever Jumbo comes round to supper, he nudges her in the ribs and says, 'How are you coping with the old dog then, little Diana? Managed to tame the rogue, eh?' She's restricted his visits to once a month, just to please Andrew. 'Come on, Di, good old Jums isn't a bad soul. Bit lonely I think, hasn't got the comfort of a wife and family like lucky me. All he'll want is a bit of shepherd's pie, no trouble at all, really.'

Diana forbears to say that shepherd's pie is a hideous amount of trouble, and the grated cheese on the top is burnt by the time Jumbo turns up, rolling through the door with lunch still fresh on his tie. He then drops ash on the carpet, just as Diana is explaining crisply that it's a non-smoking household because of Beatrice's asthma. 'Now, how is little Beatrice? Am I her godfather? Must have been a damn fine christening – can't remember a thing about it.'

Thus he settles heavily into Diana's favourite chair (it creaks omi-nously) and appropriates the 12-year-old malt. He never knows when to leave. Diana says she won't have him to a dinner party again since the time he fell asleep at the table, only waking during the main course to ask for the bill.

The Auction House
Receptionist

PETUNIA VON SELZING has a mind uncluttered by knowledge. She's touchingly aware that something rectangular is a painting, but handed a Polaroid of a William and Mary tallboy, or anything ominously oriental, and she telephones the works of art department. Petunia did take a GCSE in history of art at St Mary's Ascot, but it was only because she couldn't face the biology practical. She has led a sheltered life, brought up in a Swabian castle, holidaying only with her mother's English relations, and now works at Christoby's, a finishing school to which one can wear Ferragamo shoes. Her father knows Lord Alverstoke, and Petunia's young man, Philippe d'Uzes, works in porcelain, so it's like a cocktail party really, and sometimes the clients can be quite a bore when they interrupt conversations with her girlfriends who've popped down from Vogue House. But Petunia has immaculate manners, which enabled her to overcome her horrified surprise when someone first presented her with a toy Noddy car. She did not know that such things existed. David, the rock'n'roll specialist in the collectors' department, has tried to explain the value of pop culture to her, but there was never very much of it in Swabia, and Disney memorabilia makes Petunia clutch at her pearls.

Sometimes the pressure of being asked for an opinion – which there is absolutely no risk of her being able to give – makes her feel rather overcome, or maybe it is the smell of bruschetta with roasted garlic wafting towards the front counter from the Christoby's café. Some day soon Philippe will propose – he has a ravishing château in Provence, so blissfully warm after Germany – their parents will be delighted, and Petunia will give up work quite unaware that she has briefly stood at the socio-cultural crossroads of the twenty-first century: old money attempting to sell things and new money ravenous to buy.

*Petunia has immaculate manners, which enbled her to overcome
her horrified surprise when someone first presented her with
a toy Noddy car*

The Minicab Driver

HUSSEIN HAS A wonderful new short cut to Heathrow, a scenic route along parts of the A4 known to few and punctuated with agonisingly slow traffic lights. The porky businessman perspiring in the rear of Hussein's beige Ford is about to miss his plane to Munich. Luckily Hussein is oblivious to the resultant stream of invective, since speaking idiomatic English is not an essential qualification for working at Kozy Kabs. The H-reg Sierra smells of cigarettes, overlaid with air freshener from the little green pine tree jiggling on the dashboard. Passengers sink with an ominous creak into the springless Dralon of the rear seat, and their desperate directions are obliterated by the crackling intercom and Kiss FM. Hussein rarely listens to the traffic reports which might ameliorate his magnetic attraction to areas gridlocked by burst mains and spilt loads.

At the weekend he drives his wife, his cousin and their children to Legoland, spending a familiar four hours heaving in a traffic jam. This worries Hussein not at all, he is in England with all his family, he has a semi-detached house with a three-piece suite on hire purchase, his car is his castle and he is king of the road.

The H-reg Sierra smells of cigarettes, overlaid with air freshener from the little green pine tree jiggling on the dashboard

The Couple Who Have
Moved to the Country

GERALD IS KNACKERED. He gets up at 5.30am every day in the pitch dark to drive to Potterton station for the fast train to the City, returning each night – also in Stygian gloom – at 9pm gasping for a stiff whisky. Before you can say Jeremy Paxman he is asleep in Nina's roast pheasant with quince cheese. Nina is thriving at The Chantry House. Wandsworth seems but a dim memory and she's now the sort of woman who only goes to London to have her hair cut. She's become a bridge fiend, reads seed catalogues with an avidity normally reserved for Ruth Rendell, and keeps ornamental hens. She is entranced that the local butcher not only delivers but also makes his own pork pies – 'They're still warm from the oven,' she cries, while handing round home-made chutney at Gerald's shooting lunches. Bright-eyed with fresh air, whip-cord thin from labouring lovingly over the herbaceous border, Nina is the pastoral idyll personified. Gerald, bloated from the sedentary routine of commuting, feels that he has been reduced to the status of a contractor who cleans the swimming-pool.

There's a halcyon spell in summer when Gerald's mole-like existence is relieved by crisp dawns, balmy evenings and the fecund sight of the acres his money has earned him. It is then that Nina asks masses of people to stay. Soon he'll be on the slippery slide to a little flat in London – just a few nights a week – and Nina will be lunching in the Poacher's Arms with the gentleman farmer from Shafto Manor.

*Nina is the pastoral idyll personified. Gerald, bloated from the
sedentary routine of commuting, feels that he has been reduced
to the status of a contractor who cleans the swimming-pool*

'We haven't been flossing now, have we?' is her battlecry

The Dental Hygienist

VALERIE IS A zealot, her mission in life to rid the world of gum recession. Flexing her latex gloves in an antiseptic eyrie above Mr MacAndrew's practice, for many of her patients she is an all too vivid reincarnation of matron. 'We haven't been flossing now, have we?' is her battlecry as she grouts out oral detritus with evil steel tools. 'Now, do have a jolly good rinse.' Those not already mortified by the amount of rubble and blood in the little porcelain basin will, when prone and helpless in her chair, be lectured on the necessity of paying proper attention to their back molars. 'You really must get in there every night,' she says, 'because we don't want Mr MacAndrew to have work to do, do we?' And the words 'root canal treatment' hang in the air like a dental Armageddon. Mr MacAndrew, a dashing Australian, is Valerie's lode-star, the George Clooney of teeth, and she the self-appointed bulwark between him and the unpleasant consequences of plaque.

Those who ignore Valerie's strictures are sure to be severely cautioned on future visits when she'll take one look in their mouths before donning hideous Perspex goggles. The combination of these with her uniform, and the navy tights that make her legs look like two throbbing varicose veins, can be a bit much for those of a nervous disposition. But Valerie is a kind soul – she has a cat at home in Putney – and can detect the unfortunates who need a codeine. 'There we are, all polished,' she says comfortingly as they leave. 'So we are going to remember to floss now, aren't we?'

The Fly Fisherman

IT IS THE Mayfly season, and the most gloriously happy time of year for Peter Godolphin. He and the dogs are alone on the Kennet, the trees are in the first flush of spring green, the bees are a-buzzing and Lady Godolphin is fruitfully occupied elsewhere with the cricket teas. Now the afternoon (nicely cloudy) stretches before him, crisp with the anticipation of a gladiatorial duel between the trout and Nancy Astor, a fly Sir Peter made himself from the trimmings of a hat his wife wore last year to the King George and Queen Elizabeth Stakes.

Prior to this day of days he has been casting on the lawn, the line looping gracefully over the greenhouse and the peony bed. 'Counterpoise' and 'the fulcrum point' are issues that worry Sir Peter mightily: how did R.C. Leonard break all distance records in 1889, casting without a reel at all, the line merely coiled at his feet? 'I don't know, dear,' said Lady Godolphin, deep in a seed catalogue. So now Sir Peter is trying a lightweight reel using a weight-forward line: the problem remains, however, that trout are clever little devils, see him coming – even as a boy he remembers that casting into the weir wasn't all skittles.

Still, the lure of a mown beat, his annual days on the Test, the swish of the line and the companionship of fellow fishermen are to him the warp and weft of an English summer. In a madly adventurous moment he thought about Montana – his daughter having taken him to *A River Runs Through It* – but Lady Godolphin said that she didn't really think America was for her, and who would look after the dogs? So Sir Peter ties his own flies, floats them in the bath and submerges himself to see if, from below the water line, they look sufficiently seductive to his wily adversary, the trout.

The lure of a mown beat, his annual days on the Test, the swish of the line and the companionship of fellow fishermen are to him the warp and weft of an English summer

*It is only a matter of time before Oriole is asked
to be a Booker Prize judge*

The Hampstead Intellectual

ORIOLE'S BOOK, *Mythopoeia in Modern Society*, has received a gratifying number of reviews by her friends who write for the nation's literary pages. Even the dons who palpitate with erudition in North Oxford have been struck by her elegant deconstruction of Our Lady of Lourdes, not to mention the chapter on the mystical-feminist implications of the miniskirt. It is only a matter of time before Oriole is asked to be a Booker Prize judge. Meanwhile she is writing a paper on 'Eclectic Empiricism – or how a woman does what she does in order to get by', to be delivered at Hicksville University, Wisconsin.

Her feminism is of the sort that stands firm on iron-grey hair but is not averse to dévoré velvet shawls, or startling necklaces with heavy pendants from the Lesley Craze Gallery, Clerkenwell. In her study, a book-filled attic overlooking Hampstead's rooftops, a nude drawing of Oriole is wedged between Hobsbawm and Bettelheim; it was done while she was at Oxford, at the time she rejected Catholicism in favour of spiritual freefall. A less successful bronze head is used as a doorstop by her husband, whose study is in the basement, and he occasionally pelts it with screwed-up paper balls of his work in progress – twelve impenetrable novels that have failed to elicit first-class flights to America or visiting fellowships. He and Oriole meet sporadically in the kitchen for brown, pulse-laden food but neither believes in washing up; it would take far too much time away from their valuable work.

The Polo Player

CARLOS, HOT OFF the Pampas, only has two words of English, which are 'Leave it!', shouted just as his patron is about to hit the ball. This is when Carlos thunders up behind and scores the perfect goal, a showy performance that underwrites the handy phrases he rapidly acquires, such as 'I won't play at Cowdray unless I have helicopter transport from London'. A muscled meteor of testosterone, Carlos prefers the glitzy environs of the Royal Berkshire, which pulsates with young flesh and new money. Ideally he wants the patrons and their women to be competing for his services, so that a Porsche may be written into his next contract together with first-class flights from Argentina for his cousin Manuel to come over as groom. And then, of course, his brother Juan is progressing well as a seven-goal player. The patron's daughter is demented with joy at the idea of Carlos in triplicate and persuades Daddy, a portly international financier, about the chic of employing an entire family to mastermind his high-goal success. Naturally Carlos's father breeds the only ponies strong enough to carry him to victory.

Meanwhile Carlos's party stamina is being severely tested with Dom Perignon, and an entire new wardrobe has materialised from the kindness of blonde strangers: shopping in Ralph Lauren he never, ever says 'Leave it!' His gratitude is enthusiastic and although surprised by the English woman's penchant for hay bales rather than Egyptian cotton percale sheets, Carlos is only thankful that she does not carry a gun and is too lazy to produce anything for breakfast, even croissants.

*A muscled meteor of testosterone, Carlos wants the patrons
and their women to be competing for his services*

The London Schoolgirl

ANNA HAS GOT a *real* crisis; she's having to spend the weekend at her parents' boring house in the boring country and she's left her pager at home in Chelsea. God, it's *so* boring. Her best friend Soraya might be trying to get through to her from Accessorize on the King's Road, it's really trag because there's this really great silk bag Soraya was going to look at for her. Ringing Soraya's mobile, Anna discovers that she's actually in Pucci Pizza having bought lime-green nail varnish in Mac. God, Soraya's so lucky, all Anna wants to do in life is mooch down King's Road and go and see *Scream 10* at the cinema. Oh, and do art for GCSE because Mr Barrett is so cool, he takes school trips to the Louvre on Eurostar. Soraya's mother took her to Paris and they stayed at a really swanky hotel and Soraya went to Sephora and had her make-up designed by a computer and tried all the scent.

At Christmas Soraya's going to Mauritius. As one of only three English girls left in her class – the rest having gone to Heathfield – Anna is in the slipstream of modern Eloises. 'Lady Margaret's is so international,' her mother tells friends, while being secretly appalled by half-terms in Dubai, and the Gucci rucksacks American mothers give the headmistress at the end of term. And if Anna doesn't have at least seven pieces of clothing from Tommy Hilfiger she says no one will ever take her to the Party in the Park and she just has to see Precious ('They're a girl group, Mummy, Robbie's *so* not now'). Anna's father has just discovered she bought Marlboro Lights on the account at the newsagent, so he's cancelled her magazines – *Bliss, J-17* and *Vogue* – for a month. It's trag. For her birthday Anna's going to take Soraya and Topaz round London in a limousine and they'll all talk about pretend boyfriends.

*All Anna wants to do in life is mooch down King's Road
and do art for GCSE because Mr Barrett is so cool*

The Man from Systems

KEITH IS A modern Knight of the Round Table. Normally, Vanessa in creative marketing wouldn't contemplate a man in a drip-dry, short-sleeved shirt and a rayon tie, let alone anyone called Keith, but as her spreadsheets head towards the planet for lost computer files he assumes the allure of Sir Lancelot. 'Coffee, tea or me?' she trills encouragingly as he moves the mouse around her mat. 'Well, love,' he says, 'what you've got here is a B-line fault, so I'm going to click on the restart button.' Vanessa couldn't care less whether he does handstands on her keyboard as long as her proposal for Sushi Wong restaurants can be retrieved from the ether of technological meltdown. Keith is patient and kindly: he explains to her about reviewing her preferences and reconfiguring her safe options. At this point Vanessa would snog him – anything provided her screen flickers from a state of paralysis into the vivid life of 'tools', 'windows' and 'format'.

At home in Plaistow, Keith will say to his wife, 'That Vanessa, she's a one,' before going off to play bowls in the county championship where his persona as the life-saver of modern young women is discreetly concealed by white flannels. Tomorrow he will just pop up to check creative marketing's terminals; there could be a problem with the hard drive. By then, no longer hyperventilating with crisis, Vanessa is airily dismissive. Keith fears that her boyfriend has been teaching her subversive practices on his laptop, and now empowered with the knowledge to zap her parameter RAM, she won't need the saviour from systems.

'What you've got here is a B-line fault, so I'm going to click on the restart button.'

She had so many Army boyfriends she was known as the Regimental Mattress

The Aged Sexpot

BRONWEN WAS CONSIDERED rather fast in the Fifties: rumour had it that she kissed a boy in a taxi on her way home from a dance. And then she had her portrait painted by Nicholas Egon – louche choco-late box, dear – in that grubby little studio off King's Road. Maybe it was her handspan waist, or the luminous pictures in *Tatler* of Bronwen modelling tweeds – the knowing smile and liquid eye implying the stockings beneath – but other women never liked her. This didn't matter when men were plentiful, when so many roses arrived daily that she just tossed the yellow ones to the maid, when she had so many Army boyfriends she was known as the Regimental Mattress, when there was always a table for her at the Mirabelle.

Now all the men have died or gone to their country estates (same thing), or remarried (her husbands), and Bronwen is alone in her stolid redbrick flat in Chelsea. It's handy for dashes on the 22 bus to Waitrose for smoked salmon, the only food she understands since it does not have to be cooked. Her companions aren't neighbours but *Neighbours* (rather loud as she's a little deaf) and it doesn't matter if it's common, because it's foreign. An Algerian manicurist comes fortnightly to paint her toes – of all Bronwen's excesses, vanity has survived undiminished. One is nothing without the peep-toed sandal, the scarlet lipstick seeping into the crevices of the mouth, the dark glasses that conceal glaucoma. On the bus she thinks, 'What shall I do about my crow's feet? Buy them little velvet slippers?'

The School-run Mother

CAROLINE IS LATE. Although Nanny Michelle had cleaned the children's shoes and lined them up in the kitchen – together with Hugo's PE bag, Katie's clarinet and Nicholas's judo clothes – the dog plundered a snack-box of chicken drumsticks intended to sustain Lucy after swimming and, still smarting from being The Mother Who Forgot Boxed Drinks for the School Trip to Stonehenge, Caroline had to make sandwiches.

Now she scatters villagers to left and right, thundering through Little Ditherington in her enormous Sioux Jeep while chanting the seven times table and simultaneously conducting a spelling bee. As the vicar leaps back from the kerb into the relative safety of the newsagent, Lucy asks Hugo whether babies come out of Mummy's tummy button. Caroline, brisk in jodhpurs (she is going on to riding), deflects this line of enquiry with a nit interrogation. Did Katie use the Mother Earth aromatherapy oil for headlice prevention last night? The headmaster has written a stern letter saying it's felt that there is not enough support from parents in the continual battle against headlice. Caroline regards nits as a personal affront and James Fanshawe certainly cannot come on her school run until his threadworm has cleared up. 'What is threadworm, Mummy?' 'It's itchy bottom, silly, and James's poo wiggles,' says Hugo.

Caroline screams into the school car-park where Pippa Winslade, calmly early because her son has trumpet lessons, is looking toned in shorts and a sweatshirt (she's going on to tennis). They whinge competitively about the driving time their children's education takes: Pippa does four hours a day now because of the extra journey to retrieve Marcus from choir. This is when Caroline realises Lucy has left her sandwiches in the glovebox.

Caroline thunders through Little Ditherington in her enormous Sioux Jeep while chanting the seven times table and simultaneously conducting a spelling bee

*It is selfless that he's in bed; one doesn't want to give
these bugs to others*

The Man with a Cold

IT STARTED WITH a barbed-wire throat. William feels as if he has swallowed razor blades and there is clearly something wrong with the thermometer because he hasn't got a temperature. He has shaken it vigorously, but the mercury stubbornly refuses to nudge 99 degrees. It is really very annoying when his forehead feels so hot. He undoubtedly has a temperature, it is just that he cannot keep the thermometer in his mouth long enough to record it because of the coughing. The virus – it cannot possibly be just a cold – has probably gone to his chest. Every time he sneezes, William takes the precaution of inspecting the contents of his handkerchief. At the first intimation of yellow phlegm he will have to go to the doctor for antibiotics since clearly his mother's Lemsip and honey remedy hasn't halted his progress to an early grave.

He knows exactly where he caught it; there was a man who blew his nose on the Piccadilly line between Knightsbridge and Green Park. That must have been it. The very next day the barbed-wire effect set in and he distinctly felt a tickling in his throat at Stiggy Catchpole's drinks party in the Turf. And there was a nagging ache in his lower back, so he'd had to wave away a tray of champagne in favour of strong whisky. He went to the office the next day, but what with the headache and his swollen glands it was a supreme effort getting to grips with the Snow Fun account. His assistant, Carrie, told him to take echinacea like what she does, but she's a non-smoking vegan and had fourteen days off sick last year. Frankly, it is selfless that he's in bed; one doesn't want to give these bugs – viruses, chicken 'flu, the Taiwan Trotsky – to others. William's dog is furious, concurring with William's father's view about the cure-all of good, sharp walks. William's girlfriend, Virginia, says that colds ('And it is only a cold, not a news item that will fascinate Kirsty Young') are very common.

*Sylvia Anstruther's mouth has remained pursed up like a cat's bottom
throughout Christmas, opening minimally for little sips of sherry*

The Mother-in-law

IT WAS WHEN she arrived at the Manor Farmhouse and her youngest grandchild asked artlessly whether she'd left her broomstick at the door that Sylvia Anstruther's mouth pursed up like a cat's bottom. It has remained so throughout Christmas, opening minimally for little sips of sherry. 'Just a small glass, Mark, dear. I hardly drink, as you know, but the cold is so bitter, my poor old bones, and Dr Simpson says that, in extremis, it helps my circulation.' Mrs Anstruther has the fragility of the steel-willed. Were the house to be any hotter, she would be volubly appalled by Amanda's profligate waste of her son's hard-earned money. ('He commutes from Basingstoke, just so that she and the children can have country lives. Although one can hardly call Hampshire the country – no moors.')

Amanda, derailed by four-year-old Jack's injudicious interpretation of her 'Your mother is a witch' hysteria pre-Christmas Eve, over-compensated by stuffing Mrs Anstruther's stocking with Floris and crying quietly while mopping up the dog's sick in the study. The turkey was dry – 'Our cook always put J-cloths soaked in melted butter over the breast, dear, you should try it' – and Amanda's present from Mrs Anstruther was Delia Smith's *How to Cook*. What her daughter-in-law will never know is that, when Sylvia Anstruther returns to her bridge four in Easingwold, she will tell everyone what a wonderful Christmas she has had.

The Bachelor Cook

THE SHOPPING ALONE is a four-act play. First Ivan makes a pilgrimage to La Fromagerie in Highbury Park, where he can be confident of getting unpasteurised English cheese; the San Francisco sourdough bread has to come from Baker & Spice in Knightsbridge; the grouse from Allen's in Mount Street; and the only place he can possibly contemplate buying chocolate truffles is at Sally Clarke's in Notting Hill.

The preparation of dinner for six involves forty-eight pans, a hand-turned olivewood pestle and mortar, and a special sieve (essential for the pumpkin and amaretto tortelli) so finely meshed it's hell to wash up and has to be dried in the oven. This means none of the plates can be warmed. The pan-fried apple tart with basil, lemon and walnuts proves rather more complicated than Ivan thought, so the table isn't laid and the game chips have burnt in the goose fat he brought up from Devon. As guests arrive, he is chopping onions in the patent way taught at Leith's evening classes – a process more complicated that an art installation at Tate Modern. Spectacles fogged, Ivan sloshes out reckless quantities of very good wine. Thus no one minds that the kitchen looks like Armageddon, dinner isn't until 11 and the grouse is raw under its armpits.

The pan-fried apple tart with basil, lemon and walnuts proves rather more complicated than Ivan thought, so the table isn't laid

Piggy would regard it as extraordinarily vulgar to mind whether he won or lost his weekly round with Bertie Pfinch

The Old-fashioned Golfer

PIGGY SPOONER'S WOODS are wood, the clubhead of his putter is brown with rust and he inherited his pre-war leather canvas golf bag. A stranger to the tartan trouser, Piggy resolutely wears his shooting clothes to the Royal and Ancient St Mordred's, to which he belongs because it is one of the few links that allows dogs. Piggy regards golf as a mildly amusing way of taking a walk, and a walk would be pointless without his labrador, Semtex, wouldn't it? Semtex's destructive capabilities thrive in the rough. Thus many pleasant afternoons are spent in justification of a restorative gin tinkling at the 19th hole: 'A large one, please, Maureen, and what will you have for yourself, dear lady?'

As he inherited a comfortable amount of money and had a job in the City during the balmy days of the old boy network, Piggy has led a charmed life free from stress or any need to compete; he would regard it as extraordinarily vulgar to mind whether he won or lost his weekly round with Bertie Pfinch, although it is noticeable that on the days he wins, Maureen may benefit from a second snifter. But Piggy belongs to the world of the inspired amateur, an inverted snobbism perfected to the extent of considering anyone who didn't top their ball at the first tee to be a frightful swot.

His home life is a haven of herbaceous borders, sound shepherd's pies and a competent wife called Lavender, who was a symbol of excellence as the ladies' captain. Nothing on God's earth would ever induce Piggy to wear one of those Pringle jummys.

Leonora often muses, while colour-coding her pashmina collection, that people just worry unnecessarily

The Smug Couple

ANDREW AND LEONORA bought their five-storey house in Notting Hill long before the property boom. Since the film they have smiled self-deprecatingly and said that it's really too fashionable for them now, but it would be a shame to move when the children love the communal garden so. The neighbours have been complaining about parking difficulties since all the nannies got Mercedes people carriers, but Andrew's driver seems to have no problems. Leonora often muses, while colour-coding her pashmina collection, that people just worry unnecessarily. Only the other day her sister Imogen had a dreadful flight to New York, and Leonora couldn't understand it. When she and Andrew travel on BA, they're always upgraded to first because he has a Premium card.

At dinner parties she listens (her Michaeljohn haircut looks particularly good when her head is tilted to one side) to other parents talking about their children's dyslexia and then says gently that Flora has just won the English prize, and has such a lovely voice that she's singing the lead role in the W11 Children's Opera in December. Andrew, a loving hand upon his wife's shoulder, adds that Nicholas is a King's Scholar at Eton. When they've left ('Must go, old chap, early start – I'm a member of the working classes!'), the other couples have another reckless drink to assuage their fury that a scholarship has been lavished upon the son of a man who has just pulled off a £30 million Silverman Fuchs deal.

On Friday mornings Leonora will drive down to Hampshire with boxes of lilies from Covent Garden because she does love to do the flowers for the weekend. Andrew and Flora come by helicopter in time for a simple supper of smoked salmon and roast partridge prepared by the housekeeper. Leonora has done her Christmas shopping, and she and Andrew are the only people in the county to have retained staff for New Year's Eve.

The Terrier Breeder

JOYCE, WHEN A plain and dumpy child, was given a Poppet terrier by a kindly godfather and it proved to be her first and only love affair. The wriggly bundle of pugnaciousness and unparalleled hideousness was to her a thing of joy and beauty forever. By squirreling away her pocket money she bought Jacko a wife, Maud ('So that you can take her into the garden, eh Joycie?' said her father, as he reviewed the myriad holes dug in his lawn) and thus founded a dynasty of little Poppets that have since made her the Poppet queen of the south-east. Her Surrey farmhouse, which consistently smells of chicken thighs on a rolling boil, is home to some thirty-five terriers who utilise the sofas as assault courses and terrorise the postman. Nursing mothers sleep in Joyce's bedroom, teenage puppies by the Aga and the elderly on the bed, their stout bodies cushioned by voluminous folds of floral duvet.

Jacko, who once took first prize in the church fête's comical dog show, has long since gone eternally rabbiting but his progeny are much sought after by the new country folk in Mitsubishis who have exchanged Fulham for leafy Chalfont St Twizzle. The banker husband imagines that a bouncy little Poppet will keep his wife and children amused, and repel burglars, while he commutes. Actually it will chew £6,000 worth of Bennison curtains and widdle blissfully on the sea grass carpets. Many is the terrier puppy who is received back into the fold. No one understands their little whims quite as Joyce does.

*Her Surrey farmhouse, which smells of chicken thighs on
a rolling boil, is home to some thirty-five terriers who utilise the
sofas as assault courses*

Her talent is to be an enabler nurturing fashions for people, tossing Ann Widdecombe together with Peter Mandelson, Claus von Bulow with Jeremy Irons, in an iridescent social salad

The Political Hostess

PAOLA IS LORD Zaillian's third wife and has every intention of being his last. Thus her exoticism, her formidable powers of listening and her social skills are fine-tuned to making him feel like a demigod. His favourite wine, Pichon-Longueville-Lalande, is always in the cellar, she makes absolutely sure that his favourite food, lamb cutlets – on the rare occasions they are in for dinner – are perfectly pink, and his favourite people are orchestrated for the Zaillians' parties, which have become the social punctuation marks of the summer and Christmas seasons. The spin-doctors' limos will be double-parked outside the Belgravia mansion – 'Alastair Campbell stands up to answer the telephone when Paola calls,' says Lord Zaillian – and inside, newspaper editors and grandees will mingle with It girls. Paola prides herself on always being able to find a pretty young thing to charm Henry Kissinger. As a fundraiser for the Royal Opera House and chair of the Cleopatra Group for Humanitarian Causes, she has a wide circle to call on, and her attention is irresistibly flattering. Those whom she takes up know that, at Paola's next salon, they may meet Michael Portillo or Jack Straw, depending on which way the political wind is blowing through her drawing-room.

Her talent is to be an enabler nurturing fashions for people, tossing Ann Widdecombe together with Peter Mandelson, Claus von Bulow with Jeremy Irons, in an iridescent social salad. Paola's mystique (she was born in Rome, or was it Cairo?) is enhanced with unquestionable style: the important but simple jewellery, the Valentino couture, the smooth hair by Alexandre, which Sir Robin Day once compared to a nightingale's wing. Paola complimented him on his book, but then she has read everyone's book. She leaves nothing to chance, ringing up before a party to find out next to whom she will be sitting, and by 8pm knowing the names of their housemasters at Eton. The telephone is her jungle drum: Paola doesn't have call waiting, she has a lady-in-waiting to field the insistent demands on her time with a brisk 'Lady Zaillian regrets she will be dining at the White House on that date.'

The Couple Crippled by School Fees

PHILIPPA LAST HAD a new dress in 1989, then Charlie started his first term at Allenby's and by the time he went to Radley, Jack was beginning at Allenby's and Lottie (the mistake, but Philippa and Ian wouldn't be without her) was on the cusp of kindergarten. A long avenue of gap years and university fees stretches towards an ever-receding dot on the horizon. Once Philippa used Estée Lauder, now it's Oil of Olay; fortunately Ian fits into his father's old suits and they bought the house in Fulham very reasonably because of the subsidence. But the Volvo is seven years old and Charlie says it's embarrassing, all the other parents have Range Rovers. Allenby's school ski trips always seem to be in Whistler and cost £748, but Jack wants to go because his friend Hugo is going. Lottie, newly at Farquhar Hall where other mothers wear DKNY, is acutely aware that Philippa's style is fossilised early Diana. Philippa says it is what people are like on the inside that counts, but this is difficult to convey to a little girl who wants a pink sequinned dress from Jigsaw Junior for the Farquhar Hall choir trip to Salzburg. The music mistress says Lottie has a promising voice, so who are Philippa and Ian to deny her the £350 weekend, with a recommended £30 pocket money?

Ian, whose insurance business is being steadily undercut by the Internet, has decided to give up shooting ('Anyway, I don't enjoy it so much since the dog died'), and the family holiday will yet again be spent in a damp cottage with no washing machine in Port Isaac. 'It's near Rock, you know, but more charming, we feel, and quieter. Ian does worry about alcohol and the young.' During the summer Philippa will scour second-hand uniform shops and Charlie will get three A-levels, but despite A grades he'll fail to get into Upnorth University as it will already have filled its quota of public school entrants.

*A long avenue of gap years and university fees stretches
towards an ever-receding dot on the horizon*

*Zorica is learning the Engleesh from large notes in loopy writing,
saying: 'Make tuna salad and baked potatoes for lunch'*

The Au Pair

ZORICA IS HUNGARIAN and arrived in Clapham after a 48-hour coach journey from Budapest. And then she immediately washed up breakfast, ironed Millie's shift dresses and coloured happy faces with India. Millie has told all her friends that Zorica is a dream, not like that dreadful lump Erika who always had monthly problems and seemed to be perpetually exhausted. 'You'll find us so easy, Zorica,' says Millie brightly. 'Now that India goes to school in the mornings there's hardly a thing to do. I like the breakfast table laid properly, of course, and Christopher has to have his bacon and eggs. Then the marvellous thing about India being at Dormouse is that it's just round the corner so you can walk, taking Theo in the pram, and the dogs, so you can have a lovely time on the Common before you go to Sainsbury's.' Millie then swishes out of the house to her tennis clinic at the Harbour Club and Zorica is left learning the Engleesh from large notes in loopy writing, saying: 'Make tuna salad and baked potatoes for lunch. India is allergic to wheat, eggs, nuts and dairy products. Please clean fridge.'

After tea, and India's supper, and bathing the baby, and laying the table for Millie and Christopher ('You are wonderful, Zorica, we'll just be six for supper tonight but all the food's being delivered from Lovely Grub, so it's just the washing-up after'), Zorica sits in her airless bedroom up six flights of stairs writing to her mother. The family is very nice; London is very big; she has booked a day trip to Stratford and a ticket to *Cats*. She plots her return home strategically: a month after her departure Millie receives a telephone bill for calls to Hungary amounting to £800.

The Jockey

JIMMY IS ON the Lester Piggott diet – black coffee and cigars – so that his face seems freeze-dried and his bottom is flat-packed. He cannot remember a time when he wasn't banting, but as his body has wasted, so his bank account has bulged. He now commutes by helicopter to Epsom, to Ascot (he's riding Sheikh Faisal's hope in the Gold Cup), and to York for the August meeting. The courses pass in a whirl of chopper blades, vivid silks and owners' wives in frantic hats to whom he is scrupulously complimentary, particularly about their horse's stamina, intelligence and turn of speed in the final furlong. He may have the physiognomy of a battered suitcase but everyone loves Jimmy; housewives only have to see him punch the air in his trademark victory salute to throw money at his chances on Pegasus in the 4.45 at Goodwood – a collective act of favouritism regarded with a jaundiced eye by William Hill.

Son of a head lad, he was born a stable rat, riding before he could walk. His allegiance to trainer Michael Flaherty has been profitable to them both, and when Inspector Flatfoot came round inquiring about the curious way in which some jockeys seemed to be wandering off a straight line these days, there were no flies on Jimmy. He's married to Lindy (but not very) and has his eye on the way out of riding now. Longchamps, Sha Tin and Dubai have all become a blur overlaid with the collective smell of horse and money. Training? Too many jockeys have tried and failed. There can be only one Dick Francis. Jimmy fancies being a TV commentator: he's had an approach from the new sports channel, Winning Ticket, funded by an Australian billionaire. Flaherty says that Lester was still riding three-year-olds at the age of 57: 'Do the same and I could try you at stud, Jimmy lad, that's the way to ride into the sunset.'

*He may have the physiognomy of a battered suitcase
but everyone loves Jimmy*

They met at a wedding, and by the time Max had given her a lift home in his BMW, Sasha had already chosen the names of their children

The Infatuated Couple

MAX CALLS SASHA his little squashpot. Sasha calls Max her big, furry bear. Entwined by the convolvulus of passion, they appear like a social Gordian knot, sharing the same cigarette, drinking from the same glass, and feeding little forkfuls of sashimi to each other in 'their' restaurant. Max finishes Sasha's sentences for her, which she will later come to find maddening, but in the first flush of the affair she believes it is because he is her soulmate. No one has ever understood her like Max; he's *sooooo* funny, incredibly sensitive, loves *ER*, and cooks linguine with mussels and white wine from the River Café Cook Book. She simply hasn't noticed that he's a compulsive obsessive about Polo Ralph Lauren shirts and still calls his parents 'Mummy' and 'Daddy'.

Max thinks Sasha is adorable: the huge eyes, the blonde fragility, the sweet cleverness of being a microbiologist. His friends at the advertising agency certainly think she's a bit of all right. They met at a wedding, and by the time Max had given her a lift home in his BMW, Sasha had already chosen the names of their children. When not fused at the hip, by virtue of actually having to go to work, their symbiosis continues telephonically, a thrilling litany of little jokes (at which they'll both laugh dementedly), guess whats? and plans for the weekend when they'll go to a polo match, lie in for five hours on Sunday, read each other's horoscopes and have lunch with Mummy in Sussex. On Monday Sasha finds she's doodling her married signature on the back of a report on ptomaine poisoning.

Roderick would consider anyone who actually approached him
for a job to be an emotional and professional cripple

The Headhunter

RODERICK IS IMMACULATE. He has an immaculate house in Eaton Terrace, an immaculate blonde wife and three promising children. He has just inherited the family estate in Wiltshire, with its immaculate decoration by Prue Lane-Fox, new Aga and indoor swimming-pool. Before Roddy joined Savage & Byte he was in the Army, a good cavalry regiment previously commanded by his father and grandfather, and naturally excelled in an environment of tradition (history was his subject, at Harrow) and discipline. In short, the killer instinct became refined.

It is the axiom of the headhunter that he only seeks to woo those already on £500,000 salaries and £1 million bonuses; Roderick would consider anyone who actually approached him for a job to be an emotional and professional cripple. Yet he conceals his withering contempt of human weakness beneath suave charm and expensive tailoring, and few resist his invitations to the ballet, to Glyndebourne, to the Stella Artois at Queen's. His social life is as accomplished as his career, his wife a jewel on charity committees, and the smooth patina of their existence is facilitated by drivers, personal trainers, Filipino maids, Australian nannies and beds on first-class British Airways. Roddy frankly can't remember the last time anyone other than the pilot sat in front of him on an aircraft.

The Self-help Addict

GAEL IS SO improved as to be unrecognisable as Botsy of the Sixth, a wobbling wreck on the hockey field and the girl who always dropped her quiche when retrieving it from the oven in Dom Sci. Gael has now shed two stone and is further withering her thighs by rolling a tennis ball between them, a technique acquired from the pages devoted to Me and My Health. During her coffee break at New Age Marketing – where she is in charge of the Primrose Oil account – Gael is inspired by the 'ultimate strategy for breaking self-destructive habits', which includes set days for applying for bank loans, buying nicotine patches, and deploying felt-tip pens to colour in a progress chart.

Now, like everyone else bent on self-improvement, she is going to learn French, do pilates, take up yoga and develop her nurturing qualities. The mantra on her pinboard is 'Vision without action is but a dream' and since Kevin gave her the heave-ho after his rugby dinner she has learnt that emotional healing is only possible if you forgive yourself. Then there is the consoling virtue of aromatherapy, the tremendous challenge of stress management: 'prioritise tasks and plan a timetable at the start of each day, and keep a watchful eye on your posture.' Gael is very into checking that she's not in a tense position. 'You have to be yourself,' say the books. Reading her book on *How to Love Yourself While Becoming an Incredibly Successful Businesswoman*, Gael is dedicated to analysing her current strengths and positively absorbing her self-esteem, while buying Philosophy make-up at Space NK to improve her spots, and repeating furiously that personal development is the modern science.

*She is going to learn French, do pilates, take up yoga
and develop her nurturing qualities*

He has seen the migration of the wildebeest, the mating of leopards and the birth of a baby elephant by night

The Safari Guide

KURT IS JOCK of the Bushveld, Sir David Attenborough reinvented as a bronzed, lean hero in short shorts. Any other man wearing gnarled hiking boots and woolly socks would be condemned as utterly ridiculous, but the hairs on Kurt's muscular brown legs are bleached by the sun and his kind, piercingly blue eyes are surrounded by lovely crinkly lines from staring towards distant horizons. He has seen the migration of the wildebeest, the mating of leopards and the birth of a baby elephant by night. Apart from in *The Lion King*, never has Africa been brought so alive than during a game drive in Kurt's Land-Rover. He is an authority on the ways of the dung beetle (much examination of rhino poo, winkling out the beetles with a twig) and the conservation programme for the Bateleur eagle. At the most unexpected moment, he will suddenly stop the car and train his vast, green army binoculars on a nondescript sage bush, wherein grazes a small, dull but rare buck, and the binos are reverently passed around.

When Kurt stops his Land-Rover for the evening gin and tonic – gun resting lightly on the dashboard, knife at his belt to reassure the nervous of Kensington – he gives a reading of the stars, the Little Bear, the Big Dipper, the twinkling satellite. Kurt's jokes are not sophisticated, but his clients, fully aware that their lives are in his hands, laugh with insane relief. Back in the camp, around the fire in the boma, he tells of the time when as a child in Kenya he was bitten by a puff adder, and how he once took John Cleese to watch cheetah. It's very dark, so no one spots the absurd tide line when he removes his Ranger's cap. All the women promise to write when they get home.

She is fully aware that her role embraces everything from flower arrangements in the officers' mess to counselling of sobbing subalterns' brides

The Army Wife

SARAH IS RUTHLESSLY sensible. She organises the moves from Army quarter to Army quarter with a precision only previously accorded to the D-Day landings. By the time the Peter Jones furniture has been reconfigured in another three-bedroom redbrick box it would be hard to tell whether they were in Catterick or Cyprus, and barely have the little Herend animals been placed on the mantelpiece than she's programming Scottish dancing evenings and coach outings for the wives' club. A colonel's daughter, Sarah married a rising young captain (the wedding photograph, in its silver frame, is on the round chipboard table covered in chintz). She is fully aware that her role embraces everything from flower arrangements in the officers' mess for dinner nights to counselling of sobbing subalterns' brides.

Roderick now commands the 18th/21st Royal Pomeranian Hussars and Sarah manages the family finances so that appearances may be rigidly maintained; hers and the children's clothes are all machine-washable, the Australian merlot is poured from the wine box into decanters for supper parties and she drives a Passat bought tax-free when they were stationed in Rheindahlen. The boys' Cotgrove uniforms are secondhand, bought at the school shop's annual sale. The baby's clothes come from Sarah's sister, who's married to a banker and lives a life wreathed in Jo Malone's lime, basil and mandarin bath essence, which makes Sarah rather tight-lipped – the NAAFI only sells Radox.

When the tenants move out of the house Roderick has bought in Wiltshire (so near Salisbury Plain), Sarah will repaint the kitchen herself.

The Lady MFH

VIVIEN BECHER FIRST rode out with the Tynedale when she and her pony were both short and fat. If it rained her father's groom, Jennings, would take them home after two hours – much to the fury of horse and rider – saying, 'You know you've got a weak chest, Miss Vivien, and his lordship says you're to go straight to Nanny and have a hot bath – after you've rubbed down Moonbeam, of course.' She still waters her horses before watering herself with a large whisky, and since she doesn't believe in ill-health ('Frightful waste of time') has vigorously challenged her respiratory system with Rothmans.

The stables at Loxlove are immaculate, the kitchen a maelstrom of dirty tack, which she cleans while listening to *The Archers*. A cauldron of tripe is perpetually boiling on the Aga for the dogs; unwary guests hoping for porridge will, when investigating the slow oven, discover instead a cassoulet of linseed, oats and barley for the horses which everyone forgot to take out the night before because they'd hit the kummel. The tea bags have disappeared under copies of the *Racing Post*. Mrs Becher wears the same suit to Cheltenham every year, good tweed, good cut, and sees no point in spending good money on folderol when she's got her eye on two new horses in Ireland. Her black taffeta ball dress deserves a long service award from the Tynedale Hunt Ball (her magnificent diamond brooches usefully anchoring prehistoric bra straps), but never let it be said that the Becher hunting kit isn't impeccable. Maxwell's made her boots, Frank Hall in Market Harborough her hunting coats and the meet is the only time she ever wears lipstick or brushes her hair – usually with the Norfolk terrier's Mason Pearson.

Sometimes, skirting a bunch of bearded antis, she doesn't know who is more tiresome: Tony Blair (who ought to be castrated) or Zara Pilcher, whose beastly horse kicks like a mule. Last season the saboteurs parked in a deceptively muddy field and Blackie Becher padlocked the gate. Now that was sport.

*Her black taffeta ball dress deserves a long service award
from the Tynedale Hunt Ball*

Philippa and Martin gaze at their infant prodigy
like two mesmerised owls

The Besotted Parents

FLORENCE CECILY ROSE has just done a little burp. What a clever girl. Daddy thinks she's the cleverest girl in all the world, doesn't he, Mummy? And so Philippa and Martin gaze at their infant prodigy like two mesmerised owls. From the moment Florence made her first appearance in the Peter Pan Maternity Unit, an event videoed by her father, no other baby has ever been so beautiful, despite looking like a screaming, scarlet boiled egg. Even her maternal grandmother says it's kinder not to look. When Uncle Paul was introduced to his new niece, he fell over the baby-stroller and said that no, he wouldn't like to share in her bathtime, and perhaps they could meet again when dear little Florence was 18?

Martin, tenderly sponging the dribble of sick from Florence's chin – 'Whose a chubby, scrummy bunny?' – tells Paul that nothing, not even getting his golf handicap into single figures, has meant as much as Florence. Paul should try it, he really should, and Philippa nods with moon-like serenity as she wrestles with the baby's nappy on a changing mat covered with pixies. Nothing but the best for Florence. Her baby book is already bulging with nature notes about her first gurgle, wisps of hair and a chewed bootee ossified with spittle. 'And when that toothy-peg comes through, who's going to be a grown-up girl?'

Every precious memento that Florence manifests is stuck into the book and Martin has bought a digital camera so that he can download pictures of her astonishing feats in food redistribution on to his computer, then e-mail them to his sister in Australia. Philippa says Florence looks just like Martin, and Martin says she looks just like Philippa, and Paul mutters that anybody who knew Florence and saw the baby-on-board sign in the rear window would be insane not to drive at speed into the back of the car. And Florence bangs her spoon imperiously on the high chair.

The Genteel Shopkeeper

AFTER THE BOYS went to Bryanston, everyone told Lucy that she 'really ought to have an interest'. So now she runs a little shop in Chelsea selling knives with ceramic handles in the shape of carrots. Her friends have always said that she's so creative, and indeed Lucy makes amusing bottles of olive oil flavoured with lemongrass. She gets the oil in gallon cans on her painting holidays in Umbria, also terracotta pots which she plants with rosemary from Herb of Grace. The mark-up is surreal, but then who in Cadogan Gardens would struggle with potting compost? Lucy is such a Martha Stewart – she sells decanters with silver stoppers filled with Fairy Liquid, kitchen chic being so essential these days.

Her memory for names (perfected when she was a débutante) flatters customers and, soothed by the burning candles, they often buy another copy of *The English Gentlewoman's Window Box* while waiting for Lucy to wrestle with the till. Her husband, a property developer, jokes at dinner parties that she's technologically challenged. 'I have to sort out all the finances, artistic types don't understand VAT – mind you, I got a marvellous deal on the shop.'

Lucy has turned the conservatory of their Wandsworth house into a furious cottage industry, drying lavender and firing fruit platters. Despite this originality, her bestselling line remains tartan-edged cushions embroidered with witticisms. Lucy has high hopes for her Christmas number that reads, 'Whoever said money can't buy happiness doesn't know where to shop.'

She sells decanters with silver stoppers filled with Fairy Liquid,
kitchen chic being so essential these days

*Crawford believes that competitive recreation is the key
to success in the workplace*

The American Banker

CRAWFORD NEMESIS III has been sent to London to rationalise the management structure at WorldCorp. This means he is going to sack a lot of people or relocate them to the office in Taipei, which is much the same thing. His wife, Barbara, is deploying a similar steely technique with interior decorators. The house in Holland Park (which they were told was the fashionable place to be) is now being made over in various shades of cream, with leopardette throws on the large, hard sofas. Crawford had all the beds shipped from New York since he is uncertain about English standards of hygiene. He is uncertain about quite a lot of things to do with the English. He and Barbara arrived with approved lists of doctors, specialists, schools and orthodontists, but imagine his feelings when he went to the knee guy in Harley Street and there was no elevator. The guy specialises in torn ligaments and expects his patients to climb stairs? Is this the famous British irony?

Then there's the mystery of the clubs. Crawford is proud to say that, as an Ivy League man, he belongs to the Brook Club but he fails to understand that its reciprocal arrangements only really work one way, and White's is unlikely to gather Crawford unreservedly to its bosom. Hell, stuffy old place anyway – he and Barbara are going to join the Vanderbilt. Barbara is a fierce tennis player (it was dealing with one of her lobs that caused Crawford's knee injury) and they believe that competitive recreation is the key to success in the workplace. Crawford has given lectures on the subject, quite often over dinner, to other American bankers, while the wives who are old London hands induct Barbara into the serpentine ways of Marks & Spencer's delivery system.

As soon as the house is finished, and little Whitney Nemesis has settled at her new school, Barbara is planning a formidable social life of charity previews and the opera. Crawford will always miss the first act to show how busy he is.

The Car Rental Receptionist

ASTRID'S MISSION AT Bumper Car Rental is to make certain that it takes as long as possible for the man standing in front of her desk to achieve his Renault Twingo. He has had a perfectly dreadful journey to Flugenedelweiss – the plane was late, the luggage lost, his wife is furious and the child is crying – and now Astrid is going to deliver the final twist of the knife in the wound of modern travel. Sir may be a gold Bumper card holder but she cannot find any record of his booking in the computer. Click, click, click. 'I do my best, Sir,' she says with gutteral charmlessness. A nice queue has now built up, and every person in it wants to leap across the desk, throttle Astrid, kick her computer and grab the car keys dangling on the little board.

At this point she smiles frostily and disappears into the back office, a grand gesture of bureaucratic obfuscation. Minutes pass. When she's judged that this torture has humiliated her clientele sufficiently, Astrid returns with the piece of paper that is the missing booking form. 'Driving licence, please.' Click, click. 'And your passport.' Click, click. 'Will you be having the Bumper Bundle super insurance cover?' Click. 'We don't take American Express, only Mastercard or Visa.' She then telephones for authorisation, implying to the rest of the queue that the man's credit rating is dodgy. Finally, reluctantly, Astrid parts with the car keys and the information that by taking the lift and crossing the walkway to the fourth floor of the car park, Sir will find an orange car in bay Q51. He is to return it with a full tank of petrol.

*Astrid is going to deliver the final twist of the knife in the
wound of modern travel*

The B-list Party Blonde

IS TIFFANY ZEITGEIST a weather girl or Bond girl? No one can quite remember since she sprang fully formed on to the London PRs' party lists by virtue of wearing a fake-fur thong at the premiere of *Guerrilla Terror*. She'd thought it was a film about apes. Tiffany is certainly not a newspaper columnist, although she has a column in the *Daily Grind* which she dictates weekly – preferably on her mobile while sitting in personal shopping in Harvey Nichols – to a hapless sub-editor called Harriet. Hers is a loosely assembled shopping list featuring Dolce & Gabbana slip dresses, Fendi baguettes and Gucci flares trimmed with ostrich feathers. Harriet, who thought a baguette was something you ate, has to wrestle this into meaningful sentences punctuated by restaurant openings: 'Dishy footballer "Knees" Upton has a thrilling new sports bar in Chelsea where I saw Joan Collins, Vinnie Jones and Posh Spice. Mash of the Day has DVD telly screens and seven different kinds of bangers and mash – and I'm a girl who loves her comfort food.' Tiffany has never been seen to put a particle of canapé in her mouth.

Since her minimalist approach to clothes is beloved of photographers, and she is guaranteed to mention all passing freebies, Tiffany has become social wallpaper. She can be relied upon to turn up for the opening of a window, sometimes with her mother. She once did a quiz show for daytime television, but found the autocue too mystifying. All that reading and talking at the same time is too much for a girl with her mind on higher things – like flying Concorde to Barbados. Frankly, she's absolutely exhausted. The thank-you letters alone are a full-time job. She needs her rest on a palm-fringed beach, preferably with a photo opportunity so it is not assumed she's in the Priory. No one understands the demands of a social life in which you are asked everywhere and know no one.